Smiles of Giles

a County Alphabet Book

Created by

Giles Early Education Project

Illustrated by

Children from Giles County, VA

A
is for

The Appalachian Trail

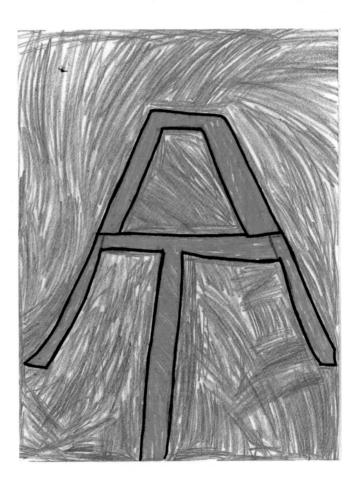

A long path crossing our land,

B
is for
Bald Knob

a very high place to stand,

C
is for
the Cascades

even a thundering waterfall,

Giles county has it all.

D
is for
Daffodils and
Dogwoods

**Springtime land
in yellow and white,**

E

is for Eagles

mighty birds

soaring in flight,

F

is for

Fishing

afternoons with a fishing pole,

free for everyone young and old.

G
is for
Glen Alton

A place in the woods

for picnics and walks,

H

is for

Herons

birds with legs

that look like stalks,

I

is for

Ice on the river

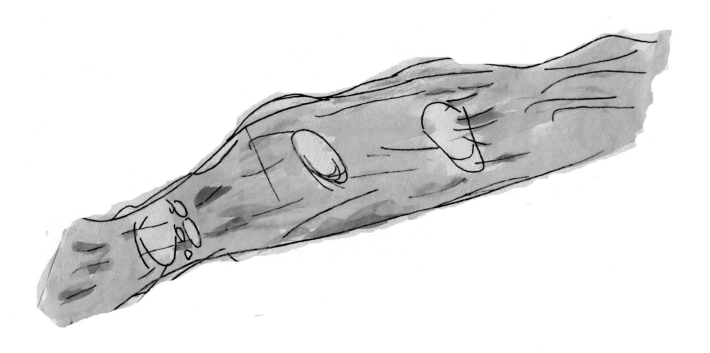

the New River in a diamond gown…

Smiles of Giles just look around.

J

is for

the Jefferson Forest

92 square miles of woods,

K

is for

Kind Neighbors

neighbors sharing garden goods,

L

is for

Lake Lodge

a mystery lake on a mountain high,

beside a hotel beneath the sky.

M

is for

Mary Draper Ingles

KB 56
EGGLESTON'S SPRINGS
NEAR HERE ADAM HARMON, PROBA-
BLY IN 1750, ESTABLISHED WHAT IS
BELIEVED TO BE THE FIRST SETTLE-
MENT IN GILES COUNTY. HERE, IN
1755, HE FOUND MARY INGLES AS
SHE WAS MAKING HER WAY BACK
TO DRAPERS MEADOWS AFTER HER
ESCAPE FROM THE INDIANS.

A pioneer woman
determined and brave,

N
is for

the Newport Fair

ponies, fun games, and pet parades,

flowers and vegetables—at the Fair.

O

is for

Old Covered Bridges

**Prettiest bridges
you'll see anywhere.**

P

is for

the Palisades Cliffs

Stone towers high and grand.

Q

is for

the Quilt of Giles

Our county's history stitched by hand.

R

is for

Ripplemead

Ripplemead Park, down at Riverbend,

float in a canoe, fun with a friend.

S

is for

Sinking Creek

A beautiful creek that comes and goes.

Where it goes nobody knows.

T

is for

Trains

Big trains along the river's course.

U

is for
Upper Narrows Falls

Water roaring with gravity's force.

V

is for

Virginia

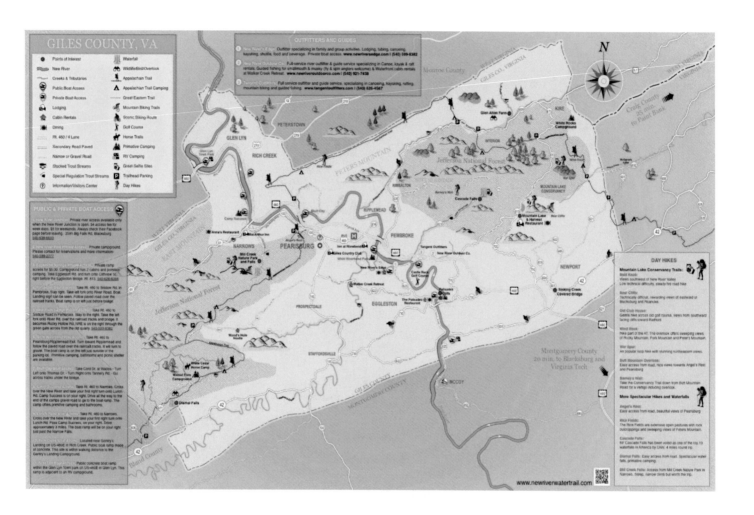

**Virginia is our state
and Giles is our county.**

W

is for

Wildlife

**Bobcats, bears, and deer
are our bounty.**

X

is for

eXtraordinary

**Outstanding art, great restaurants, too,
if you live in Giles—OH lucky you!**

Y

is for

Your County

Your beautiful county

is bright as a song.

Z

is for

Zither

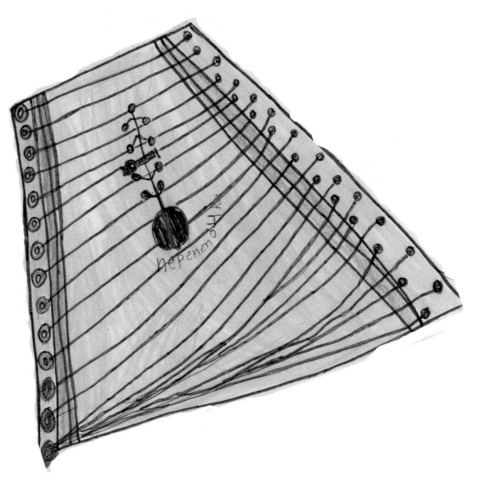

May the music of Giles

play all your life long.

ILLUSTRATORS

Paul Atkins

Chris Bailey

Jaylyn Bowles

Jouie Brewster

Abbie Brooks

Norah Brown

Elle Burgess

Hayleigh Chandler

Raigen Clark

Autumn Collins

Belle Dawson

Johnnie Dawson

Rose Dawson

Tre Dawson

Eden Denton

Hailey Dimanche

Heaven Dimanche

Mateo Dimanche

Layton Dudding

Kyra Dunbar

Jenny Dunn

Chloe Gracelyn

Jameson Hilton

Cory Howard

Chris Lambert

Jazzy Link

Payton Lovern

Landon Main

Elle Mae Martin

Sophie Martin

Emma McDaniel

Leah McDaniel

Kelsey Meredith

Ross Meredith

Tony Meredith

Darah Mitchell

Haley Myers

Alana Niece

Cara Newbill

Collin Newbill

Parker Newbill

Kian Petch

Maeve Petch

Abby Quesenberry

Nathan Quesenberry

Tristen Quesenberry

Connor Riddle

Tanner Riddle

Eva Rose Sarver-Wolf

Barbara Sexton

Jada Shrewsberry

Lynzey South

Taylor Sowers

Gavin Spenser

Kora Spenser

Leo Spenser

Cameron Spicer

Gracie Thompson

Kiva Thompson

Gracie Trent

Skyler Trent

Xyander Trent

Thacker Underwood

Jacob White

Reid White

Emily Woftner

Angela Young

Special thanks to

Ann Goette and Lynn Hill

Giles Early Education Project (GEEP)

**The "Lunch Bunch" from the Narrows High School
Summer Lunch Program for their Illustrations**

The children from LoCo Arts for their illustrations

**Alisa Moody from Wild Country Studios for her
gorgeous photographs of Giles County**

Anne and Lee Wheeler

Giles County Administration

Giles County Public Schools

Every child, a smile in Giles

Made in the USA
Columbia, SC
13 July 2017